commissary kitchen: my infamous prison cookbook

by albert "prodigy" johnson and kathy iandoli

Infamous

Infamous

Infamous

FOR INFORMATION ADDRESS INFAMOUS BOOKS, RIGHTS DEPARTMENT,
520 EIGHTH AVENUE, SUITE 2001, NEW YORK, NY 10018.

FIRST EDITION
BOOK AND JACKET DESIGN: TISCHEN FRANKLIN
JACKET PHOTOGRAPHER: SANDY KIM
FOOD PHOTOGRAPHER: TEDDY WOLFF
FOOD STYLIST: CAITLIN LEVIN
CREATIVE CONSULTANT: ROBERTA MAGRINI
EDITORIAL DIRECTOR: MARVIS JOHNSON

CATALOGING IN PUBLICATION DATA IS ON FILE WITH THE LIBRARY OF CONGRESS

ISBN: 978-0-9971462-3-3   PRINTED IN CHINA

THIS IS DEDICATED TO ALL MY
BROTHERS AND SISTERS
INCARCERATED——IN THE UNITED
STATES AND THROUGHOUT
THE WORLD——AND ANYONE TRYING
TO CHANGE THEIR HEALTH
IN CONDITIONS FIGHTING AGAINST
YOU. THIS IS FOR ALL OF YOU.

TABLE OF CONTENTS

FOREWORD

The "Commissary Kitchen" is something we've all heard about. Whether you've been in jail, visited loved ones in jail, or just watched Goodfellas, it's the incarcerated canteen filtering what those on the inside can and can't eat. Pimps like to say you control the body if you control the mind, and you better believe it's a pimp that created the Commissary. But this book is about getting free. It's about the will of the men and women in these prisons to keep fighting day-by-day recreating the food on the inside, protecting their bodies, and preserving control over their minds.

One thing that Prodigy learns on the inside is that cooking is about preparation. "I found that preparation is everything when you cook. You've gotta hook your food up when it's uncooked to taste right when it is cooked." It seems simple enough, but it's something a lot of us forget. Food isn't just nourishment; it's your being. It's your family, your memories, your neighborhood, your ethnicity, your travels, and every thing in between. As you go through the pages, you'll see that the life P lived on the outside, got him and his cohorts through on the inside.

Every single day was prep work for the Commissary Kitchen. Even "Shook Ones," arguably P's greatest hit, had a lil' gem foreshadowing the work he was about to do in the four state prisons where he served his bid. If you ever been to Baohaus, you already know, 'cause "Ain't No Such Thing as Halfway Cooks."

Eddie Huang

INTRODUCTION

First things first: this ain't no conventional cookbook. I'm not here to tell you about pinches of salt and shit or the right way to cook a chicken. Nah. Before I got locked up, I didn't cook at all. I was a world-touring rapper in the legendary Hip-Hop group Mobb Deep. I was offered luxuries like dining at five-star restaurants eating things I couldn't pronounce. My first day at Rikers, I was sent to the infirmary with food poisoning. Real talk though, it wasn't rotten food, but my body wasn't adjusted to the low quality chow being pumped into my system.

That's when I realized the system tries to kill you in many ways.

I've had sickle cell since I was a little kid, and every move I make those misshaped blood cells stay on my mind. I can't work out like you do; I can't eat like you do. I ran through four prisons during my sentence and every one of them had to have an infirmary in case I got sick. It was that serious. So spending three years in a government controlled box made me realize that the only thing I could control was how I took care of myself. It started with food.

Meals in prison are complex. You have your daily chow, but any extras come from your commissary or packages sent by your loved ones. With the exception of a few good meals, the chow was lethal. And yeah you could get a few things sent your way, but if it didn't come in a can then it probably didn't come. I had to learn to make do with what I had for survival. It saved my life.

On top of all that though, the meal prep was therapy for us. Me and the other inmates would head over to the common area and flip some meals, trying to impress each other.

Sometimes it worked; a lot of times it didn't. We eyeballed for measurements, used crazy combinations for flavors, and had only a few appliances to do it all: two toaster ovens and a microwave. But we made it happen, and some of the meals I still eat to this day.

This book won't make you a better cook, but it might make you a better person. Because in a world where prisoners are treated like animals, we made our experiences there feel more human by how we prepared our food. It was all we had, really—especially on holidays. After all, we were somebody's brother, someone's daddy. A son. This is the story of how I survived prison through the meals I ate. To the dudes I served them up with, one love. And to you reading this, take care of your bodies.

Eat up.

-P

THE BASICS

The Rules

You can't order anything in a package from the outside if they have it in commissary already. If they got it in commissary, you can't order it in a package. That's just the rule, because they're trying to sell their stuff, I guess. They had rice on the commissary sheet, so you couldn't order rice in a package. They had pasta, so you couldn't order pasta. There's just certain things that you can't get in a package if they got it in commissary. Each jail was different though. Each and every jail has different rules of what you can and can't have. They're all different, each one. So since I ran through four jails during my sentence, I had different cooking experiences with each, but Mid-State was where I spent most of my time. So that's where I cooked the most. They also didn't have vegetables in commissary, so I would have to order them.

My wife would send me 30 pounds of canned green vegetables every month (30-35 pounds is the limit). Usually when people get packages of food, they would get snacks like Twinkies – stuff that they don't have in the jail.

Whatever they was allowed to get in, they'd get. They would maybe get some sausages that they didn't have in commissary, just usually a lot of junk food type of stuff. But I would just get 30 pounds of canned green vegetables, because they didn't have any green vegetables in the prison. They only had "mixed vegetables" available in commissary. That mix was like carrots, celery, and potatoes. There was nothing green. I was surprised because it says "mixed vegetables" on the commissary sheet, and when you get it, nothing's green in it. There was maybe a few green beans in the can, but that's a joke to me. So I had to use my package just for that. If you had family and friends sending you packages or if you had money in your commissary account, then chances are you cooked, even a little. Because you get hungry in between meals. You only get fed three times a day, so in between, you want some more. Plus when they feed you, you only get served in portions. You're lucky if you know people, you can get an extra piece of chicken or something. But you be hungry. You're not supposed to, but you can save some of the food and wrap it in a napkin and put it in your pocket. We used to do that sometimes with chicken and apples and shit. And butter. We used to steal the butter from the chow. When chow would come around, they got these big bags of butter, so we used to jack the butters so we could use them to cook with. Whatever it takes to get it tasting good. Now you may see some shit in here that looks "un-

healthy," to you and you're thinking, "Ay yo P, there's mad butter in some of these recipes." All I gotta say is I worked with what I had. You think I wouldn't have cooked with extra virgin olive oil and shit if I had the chance to? Nah. This is prison.

The Schedule

We were allowed to cook any time you got out of your cell. You got up at 6am, and got ready for the day. Breakfast was at 6:30am inside the dorm. They brought the chow to our dorm, because we were in a box building, not in a regular dorm. So they brought the chow at 6:30am, you went to the yard at 7am for two hours, came back at 9am. When we got back from the yard, we used to have to carry our lunch trays up. They used to leave it at the bottom of the stairs for us, and we were on the second floor. So as soon as we came back from the yard, the lunch would be sitting there at the bottom of the staircase with a big ass thing to hold the juice, like a cooler. We would have to bring the juice up, carry up the trays to eat. Then you had lunch, finished lunch around 9:30am, then they made us lock up in the cells for like a half hour. Then you came out at 10am, and from then on, you could cook whatever you want to cook until like 2pm. Then they'd do a count—there were two counts each day: the first was at like 1 or 2pm.

We chilled for a while after the count. Dinner came around 4pm. Then you came back out and chilled in the dorm until the next count, which was probably around 10 at night or something like that. Then you gotta lock it in until the next day. We got late nights from Friday to Sunday late night, so we stayed up until two in the morning. That's when we'd really cook – all kinds of meals. During the week, 10am-1pm was the best time to cook. Right after lunch. You could take food back to your cell, but there's no refrigerator. They got a ice machine, so you could get a bucket of ice and keep it there. People used to put ice in the toilet and keep the food in the toilet, but I never did that. That's disgusting. But whatever you had, you couldn't have frozen goods or stuff that you had to keep refrigerated. They wouldn't allow it in the jail, because there's no refrigerator so it would rot and it would stink. So anything we made, we had to eat right away or it would go bad.

Survival of the illest

I couldn't afford to get sick in prison. My sickle cell is no joke, so I couldn't eat poorly or not exercise. And everything in jail is designed to do the exact opposite. There are sodium regulations that the prisons just flat out ignore. There are sugar restrictions that people don't give a fuck about either. And if all you're doing all day is laying around and eating bad food, you have no choice but to get fat and unhealthy. It's no surprise why people leave prison with high blood pressure and diabetes, even though they came in healthy. Most of the people in there though, they were trying to improve themselves. The little clique of young dudes I was running with— the hip-hop kids from the street that I could connect with—we was all on some, "We're gonna use this time to work out. We're gonna hit the gym, we're gonna be in shape!"

We was all on the same page. I seen motherfuckers lose weight and get in shape in there. We inspired the rest of the dorm, so we had everybody working out. I gotta work out a certain way because of my sickle cell. I can't work out like everybody else because it will trigger my sickle cell. So I gotta take it easy. You know how in between reps or sets, people are supposed to break for 60 seconds? That's like the norm. I gotta break for like 3 or 4 minutes to let my heart rate calm down, my adrenaline to stop pumping. I relax, breathe, then I get back. But a normal person with good health is supposed to keep going. I learned that through trial and error. I just had to figure out my body. When I would try to restart after 60 seconds, sometimes I would feel the pain trigger. And you want to move fast because everybody else is moving fast and you look like a sucker saying, "I ain't ready yet. Nah, keep going." Then they finish their workout, and you still got five more sessions to do. So I just had to get used to it. I don't give a fuck, that's just how I gotta work out.

We had to convince everyone that working out and then drinking juice wasn't the move. Drinking water was the right thing to do. We had no bottled water, though, just a water fountain. But the water in upstate New York was so clean. That was the cleanest tap water I ever drank. That was all I was drinking really. But then they would tempt everyone with a big cooler of basically sugar for breakfast, lunch, and dinner. We would have fruit punch, grape drink, orange drink, iced tea, orange juice, and apple juice. They stopped giving whole milk. They switched it, so now the whole entire New York state is 1% milk. I heard the reason they did it was because motherfuckers was getting so big. Dudes was getting brolic from the protein, and it was scaring the COs because they were overpowering them. They didn't want nobody being that big. Motherfuckers was getting big off the milk and working out, beating up the COs and whatnot, so they was like, "Nah, we gotta cut that down." That was a little rumor why they did that. I don't really know if that's true, but that's what they were saying.

Chow and the thievin' ass COs

They had a menu on the wall to see what we were having everyday at chow. Every day was different, but then it would go back and start over on like Monday. Most mornings we had liquid eggs, but our favorite for breakfast was breakfast pizza. That's good, yo. It's regular pizza with scrambled eggs on top of it. I used to tear that up. I used to try and get extra pieces and eat like two or three pieces of those. That was my favorite. Then they had "starfish" for lunch. That was the shape of it, but it was veal. It was breaded, like the cheap, nasty joint, but it was good in there. That was the only day that you got green vegetables. It came with the starfish. It was string beans. That was it for green vegetables at chow, and it only came once a week.

Dinner they would have baked chicken or rotisserie chicken, or Swedish meatballs with the gravy. Then they would have spaghetti, pizza. Other vegetables throughout the week were carrots, corn, mashed potatoes, and baked potatoes. Sometimes they used to have the little tuna in a cup. You'd peel off the top and it's mixed with mayonnaise in it

already. We'd have tuna for lunch, so we'd get a big ass tray and a little tiny ass cup of tuna. Maybe like an apple or something with it. The COs don't give a fuck, so if there was extra, you could take it.

The COs had their own food too. They used to have a cabinet with a lock on it. They had bread, salt, all types of condiments in there plus cups, knives and forks, but they used to lock it up. So we used to break into that cabinet. We used to pull it open and steal mad bread out of there and butter, salt and pepper, all kinds of shit. One time, the officers got a refrigerator, only for the officers. They'd keep a lock on it, and that's where they'd keep their lunches, their snacks. It had a freezer – it was a regular refrigerator. So one night, you know how a school has substitute teachers sometimes? Sometimes they have substitute officers, because an officer is maybe out sick or something like that, so they got some corny ass weirdo officer who don't even know the ropes. So he fell asleep in the office, and we broke into the refrigerator. We unscrewed the side of the thing, and we ate all they food, yo. We had Eggo waffles, we had iceys, we had fucking deer!

The deer up there, they would hunt. And bears! Then they could cook the meat like sausage patties: ribs, burgers, deer jerky, and they would bring it to work. They didn't have microwaves or toasters in there, so they had to use ours. And that one day we ate it all.

It wasn't like some of them didn't deserve that. This one CO. I hated this motherfucker. We used to call him Lil Pun – little fat motherfucker. He looked like a penguin, but he also looked like Pun, though. He never liked me from the beginning; he always had an attitude problem. My first day in Mid-State, you know I don't know what's going on. I had never been there before. So I get there, I got all my belongings that I'm carrying into the dorm. They showed me my cell. When I walked in the dorm, everybody's watching TV. So I pass everybody, put my stuff in my cell and I come out and go watch TV. Lil Pun is like, "What the fuck are you doing, yo?" I'm like, "What?" He's like, "Where the fuck do you think you're at? You think this is a fucking Marriott? You're in fucking prison now, motherfucker! Get the fuck back in your cell! Who told you to get out your cell?" I'm like oh, I ain't know! I see everybody

in the common area. So he's like, "Get back in your cell!" So I went back to my cell, and he's like, "You don't come out this motherfucker until I tell you to!" So I go back to my cell, chill, and then he let me out later. I wasn't supposed to come out until he said so – I didn't know that! This dude fucking barked on me. He had a preconception of me because I'm a rapper so he was going extra because of that. He was a fat motherfucker with an attitude problem.

Yo, he used to eat the chow food so there would be no extra for us. This motherfucker would eat the chow. Come on, son. Like, you in the street – why you want to eat the jail food? You could go to Quiznos, wherever you want to go, but you want to come in here and eat our food! That's what used to piss us off. He was mad fat and nasty. This motherfucker was so fat, he couldn't even see his joint. So he used to be in the bathroom and be pissing all over in the CO bathroom, and making the inmates clean it up. Because he can't see his dick so the piss would go everywhere, then he'd be like, "Yo so-and-so, go clean that up!" He never made me do that. I would have flipped out, like, "Nah, I'm not doing that!" But he used to make the inmates that he didn't like do that shit. That day we broke in, we mostly ate his food in the refrigerator, because not only would he take our food, but he brought his own. We ate all that motherfucking food, yo. But we was really open because we got to eat some food we ain't seen in years. We were like, "Oh shit, some Eggo waffles son! Look at this!" It was Blueberry Eggo waffles. We tore that up. Not gonna lie, it felt good to eat Lil Pun's food. Fat motherfucker.

Tools of the trade

You don't get much in prison to cook with. They think you're gonna wild out and start breakin' shit and cutting people, so we only got a few things to work with when we cooked. Shit is corny too, because if you really wanted to get violent you could fuck somebody up with anything. Then sometimes I just think the jails are trying to be cute, so they have to start combining things. Like a "spork." The fuck is a spork, really? A combo of a spoon and a fork so you could pierce your food and scoop it up? We got other utensils too, but that spork would creep up everywhere. It worked in our common area, especially when we needed as much as possible to work with when we're cooking, but using a spork was pointless, 'cause it just helped shovel that nasty food in faster.

What You Got

- Spork
- Knife
- Cup
- Bowl (more than one if you can get it)
- Plate
- Strainer
- Can top (But don't get caught with that shit. You get a ticket for that shit and they lock you in your cell.)
- The circled top of a can (Save that top when you cook. That's the sharpest object you could get, so you hold it sideways to chop. Don't fuck it up and slice your own hand trying to chop. You'll get clowned.)
- Straight-up toaster oven (the kind you put bread in)
- Microwave oven
- Toaster oven (the kind with the little door)
- The metal tray in the toaster oven (Now that shit will be your best friend. You use that little tray to cook everything: piecrust, baked things, fried things, even eggs. Everything. That's because that's the only thing you can use that can hold up that kind of heat. Shit is like your little private deep fryer and BBQ'er. You have no idea.)

THE FLAVORS

Seasoning saves your food. For real. Everything comes in the pen with no flavor, just packed with preservatives. So what I did was wash everything off that came in a can to get some of that toxic shit out, and when you do that it loses what little flavor it had to begin with. That's why you gotta whip up your own sauces to add to the food. Commissary has a lot of seasonings you can use, so when I give you these recipes you might be thinking, "Yo P, how the fuck did you get Sazón in prison?" And that's when I say, "Commissary yo!" You could get Sazón, Adobo, hot sauce (usually Frank's Red Hot), soy sauce, salt, pepper, sugar, mayonnaise, ketchup, barbecue sauce (that Kraft one. It's bland though so we add to it), onion powder, garlic powder, curry powder, honey. Believe it or not we get a lot from commissary, but it's not enough if you're used to eating real flavors on the outside.

That's why we add and add and add and add until we find something we like. And I don't fuck with measurements, either. Everything is "to taste" like they say in the culinary world, because everyone has a different palate. Like take me, I don't like my food over-seasoned. I like it just right, but my boys in prison wanted everything killed with seasoning. So sometimes my cooking tasted bland to them. And I'd say, "You just gonna add so much sodium and get fat in here? Not me." That's also why I don't mess with that little ramen-seasoning packet. People use that everyday behind bars. That packet has like 1000 mg of sodium in it. Imagine using 1000mg of seasoning everyday, eating food in cans already packed with sodium. Then you wonder why people leave prison obese with high blood pressure. I figured out ways to get the taste of everything without fucking up your insides.

STAPLE SAUCE RECIPES

CURRY GRAVY

- Curry powder
- Adobo
- Salt
- Pepper
- Butter (use four or five of the individual packets)
- Can of black beans

Unwrap the butter and put it in a bowl. Microwave that for like 30 seconds, until the butter is soft but not completely melted. Open the can of beans (save the lid) and drain all the liquid into the bowl of butter. That's gonna be the thickening agent, since curry outside uses flour and other types of stuff. Use a lot of curry powder. You just gotta OD with the curry powder. Add a little adobo, pepper and salt. Mix it all together. If it tastes like shit you did it wrong.

RASTA SAUCE

- **Tomato sauce in a can (two or three)**
- **Parmesan cheese**
- **Curry powder**
- **Adobo**
- **Salt**
- **Pepper**
- **Sugar**
- **Butter (use three or four of the individual packets)**
- **Can of black beans (use two if you want)**
- **Onion powder**

Take a little bowl or a cup and melt the butter in the microwave for 30 seconds. Take a bigger bowl, and open the cans of beans and drain the juice into the bowl. Then once again, you put a whole lot of curry powder. You just OD with the curry powder in there. Add in the cans of tomato sauce, then fill two or three of the empty cans with water and pour that in. Pour in the melted butter. Add some adobo, salt, pepper, and onion powder. Add a sprinkle of that sugar. Mix it all together.

HOT ASS BUFFALO SAUCE

- Hot sauce
- Butter (use two or three of the individual packets)
- Salt
- Pepper
- Onion powder
- Garlic powder
- Cayenne pepper

Melt the butter in a bowl for 30 seconds. Add the hot sauce in the bowl with the butter. How much depends on how spicy you want it to taste. I dab it until I can't see the butter anymore. Then you add the salt, pepper, onion powder, and garlic powder. Now comes the cayenne pepper. If you want it really hot, you add as much as you can. If you just want a kick, you sprinkle that in. Mix it all together.

P'S RAMEN SEASONING

(WITHOUT ALL THAT SODIUM SHIT)

- **Garlic powder**
- **Onion powder**
- **Salt**
- **Pepper**

It's that simple. Throw a lot of garlic powder and onion powder in a cup. Add salt and pepper. The more salt you put in, the closer it's gonna get to tasting real, but don't OD on it. If you want, sprinkle some Adobo or curry powder in, but don't kill it. Cover the top of a cup with a small plate and shake the cup to mix the ingredients. Boom.

P'S REMIXED PASTA SAUCE

- **Tomato sauce in a can (two or three)**
- **Hot sauce**
- **Barbecue Sauce**
- **Sugar**

Take a bowl and pour the tomato sauce in a bowl. Fill the empty cans with water and pour that in. Sprinkle in sugar, but not a lot. Add one dab of barbecue sauce and a few dabs of hot sauce. That's the trick. Mix it all together.

NO SUCH THING AS HALFWAY COOKS

Everything I learned about cooking in prison, I owe to this one dread. He was from St. Thomas or St. Croix or something like that. He was actually a chef. Yeah, that was his job in the streets. He worked in a restaurant outside, so that's how he knew how to cook so well. He didn't speak much. I think he was in there for—they were saying he was in for rape or something like that. We didn't talk to him too much because of the crime he was in for. We looked down on him. So we ain't really mess with him too much, but we would let him cook. We would give him food—like we would all chip in and give him stuff to work with—and he would cook it. We would watch him and make sure he washed his hands (that's a big problem in prison), and then we would watch him cook. After a while, I started standing next to him while he was cooking. I wanted to learn what he was doing.

He was showing me how to make sauces and how to make fish. Just how to cook it and how to make it—like, homestyle and restaurant style. He started showing me the seasoning, how to clean fish out the can, how to take the bone out. You got to be real careful so it won't fall apart. He was showing me different techniques, and eventually I started making up my own recipes and cooking them. I found that preparation is everything when you cook. You've gotta hook your food up when it's uncooked for it to taste right when it is cooked. Sounds simple, but you see so many people on the outside grabbing a piece of plain cooked chicken and then pouring all sorts of seasonings on it after it's cooked. That's not how you get it to taste good. We had prepackaged food in the pen but we knew how to prep it for cooking. That's what the dread taught me. It's probably the best lesson I got out of prison, because it led me to writing this book.

SHIT I ATE ALL THE TIME

THE DREAD'S TAKE ON A CLASSIC RECIPE

My mother always makes the bomb ass macaroni salad with the tuna and the olives or whatever. It's my favorite. So when I got locked up, I realized I could make a whole big bowl of this and have it for a few days and just eat it. So I would be in there making that. One day the dread saw me making it, and he pulled an apple out that he kept from chow and started cutting it. He's like, "I'm putting apples in it." I'm like, "Who the fuck puts apples in there?" He's like, "Trust me! Trust me, it's good. Don't knock it until you try it." And I tried it and I was like wow, it is good! I started doing it ever since. When I got out, it was the first meal I made my son. I still make it now. It's good, yo. Mad good.

MOMS' (AND THE DREAD'S) MAC SALAD

- **Elbow macaroni**
- **Mayonnaise**
- **Tuna**
- **Olives**
- **Relish**
- **Apples**
- **Salt**
- **Pepper**
- **Onions**
- **Hard-boiled eggs [if you choose to]**

Take a bowl of water and microwave it for like a minute or until it boils. Add some salt and stir. Then throw the macaroni in, and microwave it again for like three or four minutes until it gets just as soft as you want it. Strain the macaroni, and wait for it to cool or run some cold water on it like I do. Peel the apple and take the skin off, remove the seeds. Then dice the apple. We used to use the can top to do this. Be very fuckin' careful if you're gonna use a can top. You could cut your finger off. I suggest you use something else. Anyway, you dice the apple into bits, and slice the olives. Throw them in with the macaroni. Add the tuna, relish, and mayo. Add your onion, dice up your hard-boiled egg. And there you have it.

RASTA PASTA

- Rasta Sauce
- Pasta (could be elbow macaroni or spaghetti)
- Can of mushrooms
- Can of peas
- Butter (one individual packet)
- Salt

Fill a bowl with water and microwave for like a minute or until it boils. add a little salt, butter and stir. Pour in a few cups of pasta into the water. Put it back into the microwave for like three more minutes or until it looks boiling. Take out the bowl and drain the macaroni. In a separate bowl of the Rasta Sauce, add a can of drained mushrooms and a can of drained peas and mix it in. Microwave the sauce for 15-20 minutes. Take it out and pour it over the pasta. You could use this same recipe over rice.

P'S PRISON POTSTICKERS

- **Elbow macaroni**
- **Can of mixed vegetables**
- **Butter**
- **Hot sauce**
- **Soy sauce**
- **Salt**

Heat the water in a bowl for like a minute or until it boils. Add a little salt and stir. Pour in the elbow macaroni. Put it back in the microwave and overcook it until it softens how you like it. Five minutes? Six minutes? Seven? You want it gooey and basically ruined. Take it out and drain the macaroni. Get all the water out. Mush it all together so that it looks like shit. In a separate dish take the rinsed and drained can of mixed vegetables and mix in a dab of hot sauce and soy sauce. Take the glob of macaroni and make balls the size of half the palm of your hand. Press your thumb in the middle to make a tiny bowl. Add some of the mixed vegetables into the ball. Close it up and use a fork to flatten the ends like a little dumpling. Make as many as you want of those. Then, rub a half of a butter packet on the toaster oven tray. Lay the dumplings on the tray and brush some melted butter on the tops of the dumplings. Toast that for like three minutes. Flip them over, brush some more butter on, and toast for three more minutes. Flip them over again and cook for another few minutes. Some inmates liked to make the dumpling batter with wet bread, but that looked gross to me. You could also add some canned chicken to the mixture, but it takes twice as long to cook. These are fast.

DON'T BE SALTY CHICKEN RAMEN

- **Ramen noodles**
- **Canned chicken**
- **P's Ramen seasoning**

Take the ramen packet, and add water. Open the canned chicken and drain it. Chop it up with the top of the can (it comes like tuna, but still make it smaller). Throw the chicken in the water with the ramen. Add P's ramen seasoning and a SMALL amount of the season packet that comes with the ramen (just enough to get a little bit of that MSG). Microwave it for like three minutes. Somebody used to put cheese in there or something like that, but I never really did it. You can try it though.

BBQ CHICKEN

- **Pre-Cooked rotisserie chicken**
- **Barbecue sauce**
- **Hot sauce**
- **Honey**
- **Sazón**
- **Adobo**

Open the rotisserie chicken and put it off to the side. In a separate bowl, mix the barbecue sauce, hot sauce, Sazón, and Adobo. Add the chicken to the mixture and blend it all together. Microwave it for three minutes. Take it out and add some honey to it. Put it back in for another minute or two.

BAKED SEAFOOD AND VEGETABLES

- **Canned salmon**
- **Canned jack mackerel**
- **Canned vegetables**
- **Butter**
- **Sazón**
- **Garlic powder**
- **Onion powder**
- **Salt**
- **Pepper**

Take all of the seafood out of the cans, wash and drain them (be gentle with that jack mack and take the bones out the salmon). Mix the seafood carefully with Sazón, garlic powder, onion powder, and a lot of pepper. Put some butter in the microwave for 50 seconds. Pour the melted butter over the seafood and mix. Butter the toaster oven tray, and lay the seafood across the tray. Bake for 30-40 minutes in the toaster oven. Open the can of vegetables, wash and drain them. Add them to a bowl and sprinkle salt. I don't really like seasoning my vegetables. I like them to taste fresh. Put that in the microwave for like 2-3 minutes (do this when you know you only have a few minutes left on the seafood). Take both dishes out, and on a plate put the vegetables and the seafood over them.

SALMON WITH MUSHROOMS AND PEAS

- **Rasta Sauce**
- **Canned salmon**
- **Can of mushrooms**
- **Can of peas**
- **Onions**
- **Butter (one individual packet)**
- **Salt**

Open the canned salmon and rinse it, removing the bones. Chop the onions. Butter the toaster oven tray and add the salmon with the onions. Cook it well in the toaster (like 25-30 minutes). In a separate bowl of the Rasta Sauce, add a can of drained mushrooms and a can of drained peas and mix it in. Microwave the sauce for 15-20 minutes. Take it out and pour it over the salmon. Serve with rice.

FRIED CHICKEN N' THIGHS

Correction officers were corrupt as shit. There was a whole prostitution ring happening in the prison. I guess you could say the inmates were the pimps and the COs were the hookers. A lot of the inmates in there – they got game. They're from the hood, they'll be talking that shit and the girls that work there, they're from the hood too (most of them). So they'll be feeling the inmates. Not all of them were into prostitution. Some would just have sex with the inmates for free. But the ones who were down to prostitute had a whole system to it. The way they got paid was the inmates would have their family send money through Western Union. Then the inmates would pay the COs and they'd get busy in there. And they'll be having sex everywhere in the jail, in all kinds of places. It's a power thing though for the inmates, especially when you feel like you have no power in prison. If you find one of

them female prison guards who was down to fuck, you could get whatever you want from her after that. 'Cause they'll sneak all kinds of stuff over to you then: extra food, cigarettes, whatever. At least until they got caught. When I was in there, somebody had just gotten locked up. One of the officers got locked up for having sex with an inmate in the shower, and the reason they got caught is because some other inmate snitched. Fucked up, right?

I had a favorite CO, but I ain't fuck her. Her name was Officer Butz. Imagine that? Butz. And her ass was real nice too. She was cute. As far as I knew, Butz wasn't about sex with inmates, especially not for money. She was good people. But she was a little flirt and shit. She would call me in the bubble and show me pictures on her phone of her and her girls at the beach in bikinis. I was like okay nice, Butz.

One night Butz called me out to the bubble. It's a bulletproof glass bubble, where the CO sits. And then outside of that is a hallway, and then it's two dorms on each side of the hall. So the CO is never in the dorm, and we'd be in there dolo. So when you need help, the CO is way out there. Rikers Island is dangerous because of that alone. One night after chow, Butz called me out to the bubble over the microphone. I come out, and she buzzed the door to the bubble. I walk to the open doorway, and she's like, "Come inside." She reaches in her pocket and I'm like, "What the fuck?" In there, she had two pieces of fried chicken wrapped

in brown paper towels from the bathroom. She was like, "Here, eat up boy." I only had one piece of chicken from chow that night, everybody always only got one piece. They'd put it in the little window for you and walk away. So here come Butz with two more pieces. I was like, "Oh shit, good looking." Word. She hooked me up. I should've fucked her for that alone because I was hungry as hell. I didn't, though. Pussy wasn't worth stretching my sentence or getting Butz in trouble. So I ate the two pieces of chicken and walked out.

BUFFALO FRIED CHICKEN

- **Banquet fried chicken**
- **Hot ass buffalo sauce**
- **Butter**

They got boxes of fried chicken up there in commissary called Banquet. The whole state got the same chicken in their commissaries. You can get a rotisserie chicken in a package. Like on Thanksgiving, a lot of the inmates' families can bring big ass turkeys and all that. It has to be pre-cooked, though.

Everything has to be pre-cooked. Even if you get meats or something, it can't be raw. There's no freezer, so you can't freeze anything. You have to keep a bucket of ice in your cell, and if you want it cold, you gotta keep it on ice. They got an ice machine in the dorm, so you just gotta fill up your bucket and put it in your cell. Then the next day when it melts, put some fresh ice on it again. For this recipe, you cook the chicken in the microwave according to the box. Then you mix in the hot ass buffalo sauce recipe. Butter the toaster oven tray and lay the pieces of chicken. Cook for a few minutes. Take the chicken out, and add some more hot ass buffalo sauce.

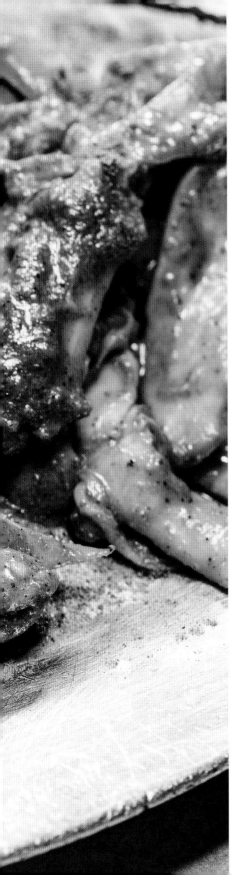

CURRY CHICKEN

- **Curry gravy**
- **Canned chicken (or canned salmon)**
- **Butter**

After you prepare the curry gravy, take the chicken (or salmon) from the can and wash and drain it (bones out of the salmon). Butter the toaster oven tray and lay the chicken on the tray with a little butter. Heat the curry gravy in the microwave. Add the chicken to the gravy and put it back in the microwave for a few minutes.

MY BIG ASS MEAL

I loved when I had visitors, especially my family. A few friends came too, but whenever my family made that trip, I made sure my uniform was tight. I'd "iron" the uniform under the bed. That's where everybody ironed their clothes. You get two uniforms, so you keep one under the bed for your visit, so by the time the visit comes, it's nice and fresh because you been sleeping on it all week. That's like your visit uniform. During the rest of the week, nobody cares.

On the visitors' floor, when my kids used to visit me with my wife, they had vending machines where you could get snacks and chips and everything that they don't have in commissary. People couldn't wait for the visit because then you could have like, hot wings you could put in the microwave! They got ill shit you could get in the vending machine. They had hot sandwiches and other food you could put in the microwave: ill snacks, doughnuts, a lot of things. Just things they don't have on the inside. They had this spicy chicken sandwich, and the name of it was Big Ass Chicken Sandwich. That was the name of it, yo! It was a spicy chicken sandwich like the one at Wendy's. It was a spicy chicken patty, it had real jalapenos on it, and it really was a Big Ass Chicken Sandwich. It was about $4 or something like that. That was my favorite thing to eat. At every visit, I would get the Big Ass Chicken Sandwich. They also had the Big Ass Burger too. It would say it right on the package – Big Ass Burger. You can't sneak it back up, though. They gotta strip search you. They gotta look in your butthole and all that. You gotta lift your nuts, cough, all that shit. After a while, I told my wife not to come because it was an 8-hour drive – four hours up to Mid-State and four hours back down. I didn't want her doing all that driving, you know what I mean? So I was like, "Don't come. Just come when you feel like it, holidays or whatever. That drive is too long." Plus in the wintertime, it's bad up there. It's crazy. You know how many times after visiting the prison, people's families would be like, "Yo, we got into a car accident and our car flipped over!" I used to tell them, "Don't come up here. Come if you really feel like coming. Don't come thinking I need a visit, because I don't give a fuck. I don't need it."

So this producer me and Havoc did music with named King Benny, it just so happened that motherfucker lived in the town where the jail was at in Utica, and he'd come and visit me every weekend. He lived five minutes from the jail. So I had a visit every weekend, and a Big Ass Chicken sandwich every weekend, sometimes a Big Ass Burger. It was crazy. He hooked me up with real kicks too. We could order sneakers, but they was corny. They had bootleg Jordans in jail. They had a bootleg catalog with fake ass Jordans, fake Timbs, fake everything, because you can't have nothing that's over $50. They want to see the receipt from the store it came from. So he used to kick sneakers under the table for me. I would buy them fake joints and wear them, he would come to the prison with new real J's on in my size. And while we were sitting, we'd kick the shoes to each other under the table—I'd put on the real J's and he would put on the fake ones. One time we did it, and we almost got caught. My man Benny is sitting right there in front of me, his back to the guards. I had to sit facing the guards. So I gotta look normal while I'm taking off my sneakers and look like I'm not doing nothing. I kicked my sneakers off, gave it to him. He kicked his sneakers off, kicked it to me, and one of the sneakers went flying to the side, almost to the next visiting table! I'm like oh shit! My boy tried to kick it over. I thought we was gonna get caught! We didn't though, but I looked pretty sus tryin' to act like nothin' was goin' on. But didn't matter, because I got some new J's. And I had a Big Ass Chicken Sandwich.

HONEY CHICKEN AND SAUSAGE

- **Banquet fried chicken**
- **Canned sausage**
- **Honey**
- **Butter**
- **Salt**

Take the Banquet fried chicken and cook it in the microwave with the instructions on the box. Open the canned sausage, rinse and drain it. Slice it with the top of the can. When the chicken is done, remove it from the bone. Put it in a dish together. Microwave some butter for like 45 seconds. Mix the butter into the chicken and sausage, along with honey and salt. Butter the toaster oven tray and lay the chicken and sausage mix on the tray and cook it until it looks glazed. Take it out and add a little more honey and salt.

BLAZIN' SALMON

- **Rice**
- **Canned salmon**
- **Onions**
- **Hot ass buffalo sauce**
- **Butter**

Boil a bag of microwavable rice. Clean the salmon off with water and remove the bones. Dice some onions. Butter the toaster oven tray, lay the salmon out in little strips. Season it up with P's ramen seasoning, Sazón, and Adobo. Put a bunch of onions around it, add more butter, and add a little bit of water so it doesn't dry up. Throw it in the toaster oven on high and just let it cook for like 40 minutes. Then you just keep watching it, and after it's finished cooking and it's real brown, then put the hot ass buffalo sauce on it. Put it back in there, and let the buffalo sauce caramelize with the onions. Serve over the rice.

FAKE ASS PAD THAI

- **Ramen noodles**
- **Canned chicken**
- **Canned mixed vegetables**
- **Peanut butter**
- **Liquid eggs**
- **P's Ramen seasoning**

Take the ramen packet, and add water. Open the canned chicken and drain it. Chop it up with the top of the can (it comes like tuna, but still make it smaller). Throw the chicken in the water with the ramen. Open the canned mixed vegetables, rinse and drain them. Add that to the mix. Add some of P's ramen seasoning and a SMALL amount of the seasoning packet that comes with the ramen. Microwave it for like three minutes. Drain the water from the mix, but not all of it. Add the peanut butter to the noodles mixture. Cook a small amount of the liquid eggs in the microwave and then throw them in there too. Add some hot sauce if you want.

CONVICT CHOPPED

When you got that much time on your hands, cooking becomes the only thing you look forward to. We ain't have much to work with, but thoughts would be running through our heads on new things to do when we cooked. And when you didn't want to eat staple prison food like mashed potato chips and ramen, your go-to healthy meals were basically all the same to start. Then you add your own personal touches. We would definitely be competing on who made one meal better than the next dude. It wasn't really a competition, but it was though. We'd be like, "Oh nah, I made it better than you this time, kid!" My favorite was barbecue salmon, but when I used to cook the salmon, I would keep it in the toaster oven extra long so that the barbecue sauce would caramelize with the onions. Everybody hated when I did that. They was like, "You cook it too long, yo! It's burning up!" But that's the only way I could eat barbecue sauce, because I don't like plain barbecue sauce. It tastes weird to me. It has to be very well done. So they used to complain when I used to make that, but I definitely made the best salmon spaghetti.

That shit was good. Everybody used to like it. I would cook that well done too – and I would put it on top of the sauce and the spaghetti. It was a pasta sauce, but I would put hot sauce in it, do a drop of barbecue sauce to give it its own flavor. Everybody added their own special touch. It was canned tomato sauce we was using, and then they had canned whole tomatoes so sometimes we would throw that in there. It was good though. One of my homies in there named Malcolm would always get heartburn every time he ate pasta because of the sauce. So the dread taught us to put a little sugar in the sauce and then he won't have heartburn no more. So we started doing that and he was better. It never bothered him again after that. I still use that trick to this day.

P'S SLAMMIN' SALMON SPAGHETTI

- Spaghetti
- Canned salmon
- Tomato sauce in a can
- Sazón
- Green peas
- Mushrooms
- Onions
- Garlic
- Butter
- Parmesan cheese
- Hot sauce
- Salt
- Pepper
- Sugar

Take the salmon out the can, clean it off with water and take the bones off. Chop the onions and garlic with the top of a can. Butter the toaster oven tray, then lay out the little pieces of fish and put a lot of Sazón on and cover it all until it looked almost like a red piece of fish. Add some onions. Then let it cook, almost until well done, like 30-40 minutes, until a little crispy. Boil a bowl of water in the microwave for like a minute. Add some salt and then the spaghetti and put it back in the microwave for like four minutes. Make the sauce separately. Take the tomato sauce, and put a little Sazón, pepper, green peas, mushrooms, and onions in there and mix it with some parmesan cheese and a sprinkle of sugar and dabs of hot sauce. Drain the pasta and add a little butter to loosen it up. Microwave the sauce for like 30 minutes. In a separate bowl, put the pasta in, then put the sauce on top and then the take the pieces of salmon on top of the sauce with the caramelized onions. That shit is so good, yo.

P'S BARBECUE SALMON

- Rice
- Canned salmon
- Onions
- Barbecue sauce
- Hot sauce
- Parmesan cheese
- Butter
- P's Ramen seasoning
- Sazón
- Adobo

Boil a bag of microwavable rice. Clean the salmon off with water and remove the bones. Dice some onions. In a separate dish, mix the barbecue sauce with hot sauce and some parmesan cheese. Butter the toaster oven tray, lay the salmon out in little strips. Season it up with P's ramen seasoning, Sazón, and Adobo. Put a bunch of onions around it, add more butter, and add a little bit of water so it doesn't dry up. Throw it in the toaster oven on high and just let it cook for like 40 minutes. Then you just keep watching it, and after it's finished cooking and it's real brown, then put the barbecue sauce on it. Put it back in there, and let the barbecue sauce caramelize with the onions. Serve over the rice.

BLACK EYED P'S

- **Canned black eyed peas**
- **Butter**
- **Salt**
- **Pepper**

My theory on black-eyed peas is to keep it simple. Open the can of peas, wash and drain them in a bowl, and while they're still a little wet, sprinkle some salt and pepper over them to taste. Throw some individual butter packets in the bowl with the peas, and microwave them for like five minutes. Open the microwave and stir the mixture. Put them back in for like another five minutes. Take them out and sprinkle more salt and pepper.

P'S SPICY SEAFOOD

- **Rice**
- **Canned calamari**
- **Canned octopus**
- **Onions**
- **Barbecue sauce**
- **Hot sauce**
- **Parmesan cheese**
- **Butter**
- **P's Ramen seasoning**
- **Sazón**
- **Adobo**

This is similar to the Barbecue Salmon recipe, but don't overcook the seafood or else it'll taste like rubber. Boil a bag of microwavable rice. Drain the octopus and calamari from their cans and chop them up. Dice some onions. In a separate dish, mix the barbecue sauce with hot sauce and some parmesan cheese. Butter the toaster oven tray, lay the seafood out evenly. Season it up with P's ramen seasoning, Sazón, and Adobo. Put a bunch of onions around it, add more butter, and add a little bit of water so it doesn't dry up. Throw it in the toaster oven and keep watching it. Don't let it get too brown (you can tell by the color of the onions) so maybe 30 minutes, then put the barbecue sauce on it. Put it back in there, and let the barbecue sauce caramelize with the onions. Serve over the rice.

VEGETABLE FRIED RICE

- **Rice**
- **Canned mixed vegetables**
- **Onions**
- **Liquid eggs**
- **Butter**
- **Hot sauce**

Boil the bag of microwavable rice. Mix in a lot of butter. Open the can of mixed vegetables and drain it. Chop up some onions. Mix it in with the rice. Butter the toaster oven tray (more than usual). Put it in the toaster oven for like 30 minutes. Every five minutes, stir the rice and put it back in. You just gotta look at it and watch it. When it starts getting brown, make sure it doesn't burn and stick to the pan. Halfway through, pour a little of the liquid egg in there and stir it around with it. Keep an eye out until it's all golden brown. Serve with some hot sauce. I remember one night I was doing it and it was taking mad long, and all the other inmates was mad as hell because they wanted to cook they food and I was sitting there making fried rice. Mad good though.

GOOD AS FUCK SEAFOOD

- **Rasta Sauce**
- **Canned calamari**
- **Canned octopus**
- **Can of peas**
- **Onions**
- **Butter (one individual packet)**
- **Salt**

Drain the octopus and calamari from their cans and chop them up. Dice some onions. In a separate bowl of the Rasta Sauce, add a can of drained peas and mix it in. Butter the toaster oven tray, lay the seafood out evenly. Put a bunch of onions around it, add more butter, and add a little bit of water so it doesn't dry up plus some salt. Throw it in the toaster oven and keep watching it. Don't let it get too cooked or else it will taste like rubber. Then put the Rasta sauce on it. Put it back in there, and let it heat a little longer. Take it out and serve with rice.

KICKED UP JACK MACK

- **Rice**
- **Canned jack mackerel**
- **Onions**
- **Barbecue sauce**
- **Hot sauce**
- **Parmesan cheese**
- **Butter**
- **P's Ramen seasoning**
- **Sazón**
- **Adobo**

Boil a bag of microwavable rice. Clean the jack mack off with water. Be real gentle or else it will fall apart. Dice some onions. In a separate dish, mix the barbecue sauce with hot sauce and some parmesan cheese. Butter the toaster oven tray, lay the jack mack gently out in little strips. Season it up with P's ramen seasoning, Sazón, and Adobo. Put a bunch of onions around it, add more butter, and add a little bit of water so it doesn't dry up. Throw it in the toaster oven on high and just let it cook for maybe 30 minutes. Then you just keep watching it, and after it's finished cooking and it's real brown, then put the barbecue sauce on it. Put it back in there, and let the barbecue sauce caramelize with the onions. Serve over the rice.

VEGETARIAN CURRY

- **Curry gravy**
- **Rice**
- **Canned vegetables**
- **Butter**

Boil rice in the microwaveable bag. After you prepare the curry gravy, open the canned vegetables and rinse and drain them. Mix them together. Heat the curry gravy mixture in the microwave with a packet of butter. Pour it over rice.

SCRAMBLED EGGS N' P'S

- Liquid eggs
- Canned peas
- Butter
- Salt
- Pepper
- Hot sauce

Take the liquid eggs and pour them in a bowl. Open the canned peas and rinse and drain them. Add them to the eggs with salt and pepper. If you want to add some sliced canned sausage here, you can, but I didn't always do that. Butter the toaster oven tray a lot and pour the egg mixture in. Let it cook in the toaster oven. Every few minutes, you just keep mixing it on the tray. Then put it back in. It's like frying it. Do that until the eggs are cooked to your liking. Add some hot sauce if you want.

SWEET AS FUCK YAMS

- **Canned yams**
- **Honey**
- **Butter**
- **Salt**

The canned yams they had at commissary weren't like the ones at a soul food restaurant, so you had to make it as best as you could. Open the can of yams and pour them into a bowl. Mix mad sugar onto them and a sprinkle of salt. Throw some individual butter packets in the bowl with the yams, and microwave them for like 90 seconds. Open the microwave and stir the mixture. Put them back in for like another 45 seconds. Take them out and drizzle honey over them.

P'S RED TUNA

- **Canned Tuna**
- **Onions**
- **Green olives**
- **Mayonnaise**
- **Sazón**
- **Salt**
- **Pepper**

Open the can of tuna and drain it. Chop up some onions and green olives. Put the tuna in a bowl and add the Sazón. It'll turn it a reddish color (depending on how much Sazón you add). Then add the onions and green olives, mayonnaise, salt and pepper. Mix that up good. Eat it on bread or with crackers.

SHIT I DIDN'T
EAT A LOT (BUT
YOU MIGHT WANNA
TRY IT)

THE DAY I FUCKED IT UP WITH MY CONNECT

Like I said, every month I had my wife only send me green vegetables. Since we had that weight limit, I would get vegetables like canned spinach, green beans, everything green. People thought I was crazy for not getting other goods, but I was on a strict diet, training myself and my body. I wanted to see how strong I was getting and wanted to see if I could really heal myself and not get sick. I had a connect though that gave me everything else. One fan, her mom owned a real famous publishing company. I was in a few of their magazines a bunch of times. So she just wrote me out of nowhere like, "Yo, what's up! I'm a fan of your music. If you need anything, let me know." So I started writing her back and kicking it with her. She started sending me nude pictures and all kinds of shit, sending me pic-tures of her and her family killing rhinos and lions, going hunting in Africa. She'd be sending me pic-tures of catching big ass swordfish out in the ocean, shooting AK-47s. She was crazy. She was also a dope fiend and had to go to rehab. One of her boyfriends got her strung out on heroin. But she was super rich.

I used to take the catalog, circle everything I wanted and just mail it to her, and I used to get big ass packages from her. She would send me jackets, boots, everything. She sent any kind of food from the cat-alog I wanted like fruit cups, pine-apple cups, and chips when I really wanted them. One time, I fucked it up with her and got greedy. I circled a Gucci watch and sent it to her like, "Buy me one of these!" That was the end. She never wrote me back.

P'S PINEAPPLE CHICKEN SALAD
(BACK WHEN I HAD FRUIT CUPS)

- Canned chicken
- Pineapple fruit cups
- Onions
- Mayonnaise
- Salt

Open the canned chicken and drain it. Put it in a bowl. Open the pineapple fruit cups and drain them. Chop up the pineapples and the onions. Add them to the chicken salad with some salt. Then add the mayonnaise. I made this a few times and then the connect stopped sending fruit cups so fuck it.

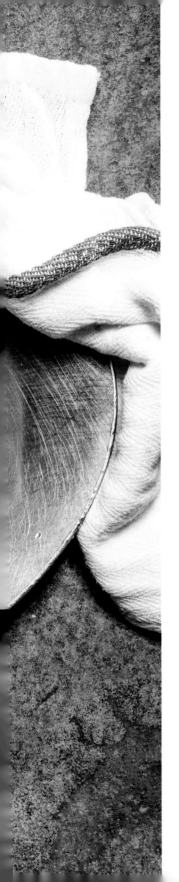

GARLIC BACON GRILLED CHEESE

- **White bread**
- **American Cheese**
- **Pre-Cooked Bacon**
- **Butter**
- **Garlic Powder**

I didn't make too many sandwiches except for peanut butter and jelly. I used to eat that all the time when I wanted a fast meal, but this right here is a recipe for another sandwich with those pre-cooked packs of bacon they sold in commissary. I remember on the outside some people was like, "Yo P did you make grilled cheese with a paper bag and an iron in prison?" I was like, "Yo we ain't even have an iron for our uniform. How the fuck you think I had one for a sandwich?" Nah, this one was made in a toaster. Take the white bread and put it in the bread toaster oven, lightly toasting it. Mix some garlic powder with butter. Take it out and butter the tops and bottoms of both slices of bread with the garlic butter. Add the cheese and bacon between the buttered toasted bread slices. Butter the toaster oven tray and add the sandwich. Toast it until it starts looking brown, flipping it once. Don't take it out until the cheese looks good and melted.

SHAKIRA'S DIRTY PIE

We had this one inmate, we called her Shakira, and she was transgender. See back then, it wasn't like that when dudes were becoming women; they were still called men. Like in Orange Is The New Black that one character got to be in the women's prison even though she wasn't like a woman, yet. If you were born a dude, you went to the men's prison. It's mad different now. But we all had the same uniform on back then. We had to wear state greens. The nurse used to come in every day and give Shakira shots of—I guess estrogen or something like that to make her tits grow and stuff. It was crazy. That's like a law, they have to do that. She was explaining it to me. She was like, if you stop getting it, something bad could happen to you. So they have to keep giving it to you. The motherfucker was cool though, you know what I mean? I ain't have no problem with her.

So one day she wanted to make us all pie. Now right in the common area was a bathroom, but there wasn't no sink in there. So when people come out the bathroom, you were supposed to wash your hands right there at the sink outside of the door. And we would watch everybody. We would be in the common area, and the bathroom was right there, the microwave and the sink where people cook is right there. Everything is right there. So we'd be watching TV and we watching everybody. We would see people come out the bathroom, and just go straight to cooking or straight to doing something, and we'd be like, "You ain't even wash your hands, yo! You touching the TV, other people gotta touch that yo!" We used to bark on people that ain't wash they hands. So before Shakira got to cooking her pie, she went into the bathroom. She got out and ain't wash her hands. Me and my boys all looked at each other. And there she went about her business making that pie.

She made sweet potato pie with the graham cracker crust. She made the crust first. I was like, "What the hell?" I never saw that before."

She crushed the graham crackers and added water, just enough to moisten the graham crackers but not soak them. She mushed the mixture up and flattened it in the tray of the toaster oven. Then she cooked the sweet potatoes in the microwave. She mashed up the sweet potatoes and put them onto the crust and cooked the whole thing in the toaster. It looked mad good when it was done, and she was all happy. We ain't eat none of the pie that she made. She was trying to offer it, and she was mad nobody wanted to eat it. We said, "Nah chill. You ain't washed your hands." She learned her lesson quick. But if you follow this recipe, you'll bake a bomb ass sweet potato pie. Just wash your fuckin' hands before you make it.

P'S CLEAN HANDS SWEET POTATO PIE

- **Graham crackers**
- **Canned yams**
- **Sugar**
- **Honey**
- **Butter (five or six individual packets)**

Crush up the graham crackers until there's no big chunks. Take the butter and melt it for 30 seconds. Mix it with the crushed graham crackers until it's like a rough paste. Spread it on the toaster oven tray and cook it for like five minutes. Take the yams out of the can (with the juice) and pour them into a bowl. Add some sugar and a little honey and mash them all together. Put the mash in the microwave for like a minute to soften it, and add a little butter. Mix it again. Pour the filling over the graham cracker crust and put it back in the toaster oven for like 25 minutes. Eyeball it to see if you need more time.

MY MID-STATE ITALIAN HOLIDAY

This one Chief of Police in upstate New York got locked up because he was selling keys of coke. He was an old dude, like late '60s or '70s maybe. He was cool. I used to kick it with him all the time and he saw that I was writing my first book My Infamous Life. Everybody in jail saw that I was writing a book. I used to let them read chapters like, "Tell me how you like that." So he was like, "Yo, when I get out, I'm coming to one of your shows or something man!" So when I got out, I started doing speaking engagements at colleges for the book. One of the colleges I went to—I think it was Connecticut—I look to my left, and the Chief of Police is there with his son! His son is like 16 or 17 or something, and I was like oh shit! He was there at the college He was like, "I told you I was gonna come, man!" Real cool guy.

He liked to cook when we were in prison, but we was always hogging the microwave, so he ain't really get to cook that much. The black dudes was always hogging everything in the dorm, you know what I mean? So when he did cook though, he used to make some real ill Italian meals using special cans of olives and special stuff. He would get it all in his package that was mailed to him. Real gourmet-type stuff, special mushrooms, and all kinds of food. He'd be standing there, chopping it all up, making sure everything was precise. He's the one who taught me how to crush garlic the right way. He was like, "Yo, you just gotta crush it like this when you open it with a knife," and then flattened it out with the side of the knife or top of a can. I was just peeling it and slicing it before. I was doing too much. He was like, "Nah, do it like this!" So on Thanksgiving, he made

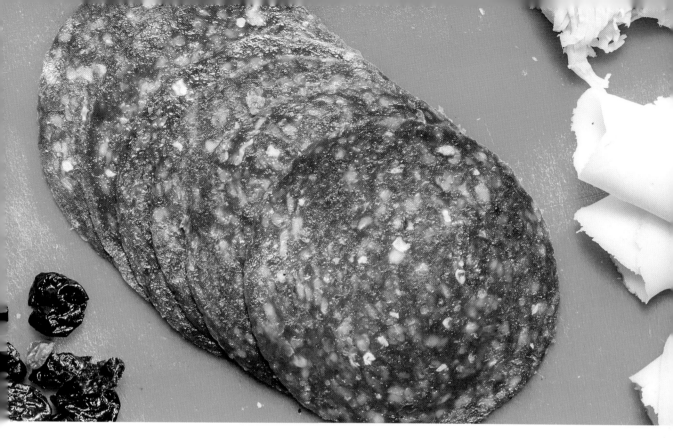

this big tray that was like from one end of the table to another. It was like a big table where he rolled out all this food—I don't know how long it took him to make this thing, but it was meats, cheeses and crackers and olives and it was all like a design. It looked like a gingerbread house or something! It was mad big! He told me later on that it was called "antipasto," which means everything you eat at an Italian meal before you even get to the pasta. It was ill. He made the antipasto for everybody to enjoy, the whole dorm. That was cool. We was all sitting around, and it was Thanksgiving so you know some people were emotional. People was missing their families, some of the dudes started crying. It was sad to watch, and I missed my family too, but it didn't take a holiday for me to remember that. I don't give a fuck about all that. Fuck a Thanksgiving, you know what I mean?

THE ILLEST ANTIPASTO PLATTER

- **Gourmet cold cuts**
- **Good cheese**
- **Olives**
- **Pickled vegetables**
- **Marinated vegetables**
- **Dried fruits**
- **Crackers**

After the chief introduced me to anti-pasto, I started realizing that I ate that more than once. So eating it there and at other restaurants and with my Italian friends, my favorite one has all different things in it. Italian cold cuts like prosciutto are rolled in it (I don't really fuck with pork, but some people love that), salami, and ham. Then cheeses like mozzarella, provolone, and more fancy items get thrown in—sometimes rolled from slices, other times in chunks. Then you got your olives in their own pile, the marinated and pickled vegetables get they own shine and you toss some dried fruits like apricots and apples in the little corners to fill in any gaps. It looks like art and if you have enough people in the room, it'll be gone in 10 minutes.

CLASSIC PRISON DISHES

Y'all know I try to stay healthy, but chances are you bought this book for some of those crazy ass prison recipes. I can say right now that I only ate that shit because I had to, but since I'm Chef Boyar-P up in this motherfucker, I remixed some classic prison recipes for you to try out. Let me say again that most of these recipes were fucking disgusting to me, but I know you wanna try them out. So here they go.

WARNING: I DON'T FUCK WITH PRISON SURPRISE

When I first got to Rikers Island, I met this one dude. I forget his name, but he was a little Guyanese kid. He knew one of my mans on the street, and was like, "Yo I know so-and-so!" And I was like, "Aight, that's wassup." So he was cooking and he was like, "I want to show you how to make this shit." He was right about it being "shit." It's called Prison Surprise in most prisons, and inmates modify it however they want. So I tried it, and it tasted like shit. Then I went to lay down and go to sleep hours later. All of a sudden I was feeling nauseous. I was like, why am I feeling so fucked up? I started sweating, like I was sweat-ing bullets! I'm like yo, what the fuck? Why I'm sweating like this? Then I just started throwing up. I ain't know what was wrong with me, but I figured something must have been in that food I just ate. I caught the ill food poisoning or something real quick, yo. So I threw up like three times, and then they took me to the infirmary and just gave me an IV. That was my first day there! At that point, I was like, I'm never eating somebody's creation ever again. Don't make me nothing. A lot of people fuck with prison surprise. I'm not one of those people. But if you wanna be stupid enough to try it, I have the recipe for you.

P'S DON'T TRY THIS AT HOME PRISON SURPRISE

- **Ramen noodles**
- **Doritos (you could also substitute with Cheez-Its or sliced cheese)**
- **Jack Mack (tuna works fine too)**
- **Hot sauce**

Open the can of Jack Mack, and rinse the fish off gently. Take a bowl of water and microwave it for a minute or until it boils. Throw in ramen noodles and stir it. Grab the chips and crush them up until they're a fine powder and mix them in with cooked ramen noodles. It'll make like a cheese sauce. Throw in the Jack Mack, and then you eat it. Good luck, yo.

P'S JAIL BREAK

- **Ramen noodles**
- **Doritos (you could also substitute with Cheez-Its or sliced cheese)**
- **Canned Sausage**
- **Hot sauce**

Break is like a classic prison meal, and it's almost like Prison Surprise but it's the jack mack in Prison Surprise that fucks it up for everyone. Break isn't so bad, but I still don't mess with it like that. Open the canned sausage, drain and slice it. Take a bowl of water and microwave it for a minute or until it boils. Throw in ramen noodles and stir it. Grab the chips and crush them up until they're a fine powder and mix them in with cooked ramen noodles. It'll make like a cheese sauce. Throw in sausage slices, and then eat it.

HOOCH

I'm not a big drinker. When I drink, I gotta move around. I like to be doing something, so I couldn't drink in jail. There's nowhere to go! I would be fucking aggravated. It's hard to make Hooch in jail, because you'll get caught making it. They do random cell searches all the time, and you gotta have it somewhere sitting there for like a month to get really good and fermented. So it's like you really gotta hide the bottle or the bag somewhere where they won't find it. They had some people doing that, but me and my peoples never really did that. I didn't want to push my sentence any longer than it already was. I watched enough dudes do it though, and fucked around with my own recipe once I got out. I still don't like that shit yo.

P'S PRISON SANGRIA

- **Apples**
- **Oranges**
- **Mixed fruit cups**
- **Bread**
- **Ketchup**
- **Sugar**

Take a big ass sealable bag and add chopped oranges, apples and the mixed fruit cups. Add some water to the bag and a slice of bread. Mash it together until it looks fucking disgusting. Seal the bag. Boil some water in a bowl in the microwave and sit the bag in the bowl. Wrap that hot ass bag in a t-shirt and hide it. After a few days, the bag should start blowing up, which means there's gas in there and it's becoming liquor. Open the bag a little and add some ketchup and a ton of sugar. Do the hot water thing again. Keep doing that every day for like a week. Then it should be done. The longer you keep that, the more fucked up you'll get on the Hooch. It smells fucking disgusting, just so you know.

P'S FIRE WRAP

- **Ramen noodles**
- **Bagged cheese chips (like Doritos, Fritos or Cheetos)**
- **Canned sausages**
- **Hot sauce**

Boil the ramen noodles in water, but overcook them until they're mushy but still have a shape. Mash up the chips until they're like a powder and put them back in their bag. Slice up the canned sausages and dump them and the ramen into that same bag. Boil water in the microwave and add it into the bag, but don't fill it, just cover the food. Fold the bag over and wrap it up into a shape like a burrito. Wrap it up in a t-shirt and leave it for like twenty minutes. Unwrap it gently and add hot sauce.

H.N.I. CHI-CHI

- **Ramen noodles**
- **Canned sausages**
- **Pre-cooked chili package**
- **Hot Ass Buffalo Sauce**

Chi-Chi is a staple in a lot of prisons. The mix doesn't seem so bad until the ramen comes into play. I would make this without the ramen and throw it on some rice instead, but let's make it authentic here. Boil a bowl of water in the microwave. Break up all the ramen noodles while they're dry and put them in the bowl of boiling water. Slice the sausages and mix them together with the chili package and add the Hot Ass Buffalo Sauce. Put that in the microwave. While that's cooking, strain the ramen noodle bits. Put all that together in a sealable bag and mash it all together. Fucking disgusting yo.

BBQ CHILI PIE

- **Bagged corn chips**
- **Bagged BBQ potato chips**
- **Cheese**
- **Pre-cooked chili package**
- **Hot Ass Buffalo Sauce**

I never understood the point of this one. They called it a "pie" but most of the time it wasn't no crust. You could mash up the corn chips and add water to make a crust in the toaster oven, but if you really trying to keep it G with these prison meals then you ain't have that kind of time for all that. So take a plate and break up the corn chips and BBQ potato chips (not into a powder, but like a fake ass crust). Throw some cheese slices on it and microwave for like 20 seconds to melt the cheese. Put that to the side and take the chili and mix with the Hot Ass Buffalo Sauce. Heat that up in the microwave and then add it to the cheese and chips. Put a few more slices of cheese on it and put it back in the microwave for a few more seconds to melt the cheese on top. There's your pie.

ABOUT THE AUTHORS

Albert "Prodigy" Johnson is a Platinum recording artist and member of the legendary Hip-Hop duo Mobb Deep. In 2006, Prodigy was arrested for gun possession and served a three-year prison term. In 2011, he released his first memoir, the critically acclaimed My Infamous Life. Since then, Prodigy has continued to release both solo projects and albums through Mobb Deep, touring worldwide. When he isn't touring, Prodigy is traveling the United States, lecturing at venues like MIT about the prison system and offering insight on changing the quality of inmates' lives.

Kathy Iandoli is a critically acclaimed journalist and author. Her work has appeared in publications such as *Pitchfork, VICE, Maxim, O, Cosmopolitan, The Village Voice, Rolling Stone, Billboard*, and many others. She is also a professor of Music Business at select universities in New York and New Jersey.

ACKNOWLEDGMENTS

PRODIGY:

RESPECT TO MY BROTHER GREG, MARVIS JOHNSON, ROBERTA MAGRINI, ICE FROM A-LIST AGENCY, KATHY IANDOLI, EDDIE HUANG, JOHN SEYMOUR, KYLE MARTIN AND THE GOOD PEOPLE AT SWEET CHICK NYC, NICK PORCELLI, TEDDY WOLFF, SANDY KIM, CAITLIN LEVIN, TISCHEN FRANKLIN, OFFICER LINDA LINDSAY, OFFICER ANDREA THOMPSON, AND EVERYONE WHO HELPED US OUT AT QUEENS HOUSE OF DETENTION, ROXANNE DANSET, ANNA POLONSKY, MY MENTOR JAY RECTOR, ALCHEMIST, MY PARTNER HAVOC, TWIN GAMBINO, BIG NOYD, GOTTI, GODFATHER, TY NITTY, SONNY (FLEE), CHRIS BARRETT, WINSTON B. HOLDER (BGOLD), JOE THE ENGINEER, CASH BILLZ, COOLR THE DON, KING BENNY, MARK THE BEAST, DJ KAY SLAY, STATIK SELEKTAH, DOM DIRTY, TYSON, NAS, JAY-Z, WU-TANG CLAN, 50 CENT. BUN B, JUICY J, T.I., WIZ KHALIFA, WAKA FLOCKA, SNOOP DOGG, BIG TRAY DEEE, DAZ & KURUPT, THE GAME, THE LOX, FAITH EVANS, LIL CEASE, WYCLEF (HIS FAMILY AND CREW), FRENCH MONTANA, GABY, OMMAS KEITH, Q BUTTA, DAN "THE MAN" MELAMID, A$AP MOB,

R.I.P. CHINX DRUGZ
R.I.P. A$AP YAMS.

KATHY IANDOLI:

THANK YOU TO PRODIGY FOR HAVING THE FAITH IN ME TO TELL HIS STORY MEAL BY MEAL. MARVIS JOHNSON, ROBERTA MAGRINI AND THE FAMILY AT INFAMOUS BOOKS FOR ALL OF OUR COMBINED EFFORTS IN MAKING THIS HAPPEN. TO MARISA FOR BEING ENTRUSTED WITH THE TAPES. THANKS TO MY MOM AND ALL OF MY FRIENDS AND FAMILY WHO BOUGHT THIS BOOK. LASTLY, THANK YOU TO MOBB DEEP FOR SOUNDTRACKING MY LIFE.

CREDITS

CHEF: NICK PORCELLI

PHOTO SHOOT LOCATIONS:
SWEET CHICK NYC AND QUEENS HOUSE OF DETENTION

PRODIGY PHOTOGRAPHER: SANDY KIM

FOOD PHOTOGRAPHER: TEDDY WOLFF

FOOD STYLIST: CAITLIN LEVIN

CREATIVE DIRECTION: TISCHEN FRANKLIN